A MISGUIDED THOUGHT

Extended Edition

JAELYN JORDAN

DJS LEGACY
PUBLISHING HOUSE

Djs legacy incorporated

A MISGUIDED THOUGHT

I dedicate this book to my fans, peers, and most of all everyone
feeling lost, alone, or seeking answers.
By Grace Through Faith!
Thank you all for not only supporting my life's work, but for
supporting Gods talent bestowed in me.

CONTENTS

CHARACTERISTICS

Changes

I'm changing, what can I say?
I'm hoping for a brighter day,
Free to speak, free to be me,
I'm waiting for a change in a world full of hurt and pain, Lives
being slain because of whom their parents chose to lay ,
To have been born a beautiful color just to be outcast, only a few
can relate.
I pray for change to rescue us all from being consumed by our
Sins and sins of others, waiting on time to change, to set me free.
Waiting on a world that can love me for me
Look in the mirror I beg of you, look in the past! Have you seen?
What I've seen?
Look in the future, what can you see?
Because without change there's nothing left of you and me open
your hearts, open your minds
Let our love flourish through time and space.

Monsters Inside

Darkness overrules me, negativity claims me, my heart and soul
screams to be set free,
En-captured by these monsters that one can't see I pray to thy
heavens, one can rescue me.
Voices in my head driving me insane,
These monsters inside are the ones to blame,
These monsters,
These voices are becoming hard to bear wanting me to steal, to
kill, to corrupt human souls how these monsters, these demons got
in me I don't know but unless I can revoke them, a human life
must go.

My Love

My love, I have tried with all my might to grasp a form comparable to thine,
I wish upon the stars at night, that you and I would grow old together, that we could see our great-grandchildren in our golden days...
I pray that with me you'll always be happy as I am forever yours.

I Pray

I Pray
I pray to the heavens you'll always be mine think of me not as a
devil but as a king, a king worthy of your love.
I see thy heart is pure and thy mind is golden, I pray thy love will
never fade for my heart can't take another everlasting heartache.

Eyes into Your Soul

My love for you so ever embers like fire in the dark,
My heart and eyes are overwhelmed by your beauty and soul I
can't help but feel lost in this world & to know that you no longer
love me kills me.
Can you not see, I'm the one destined to be with you or do you
see through me like a crystal glass , simply because you have no idea
what I feel for you?
I can't bear the sight of you with another man; I can't take
watching the two of you galloping through lilies while I'm here,
watching from the sidelines.
A cowardly fool I must be If only you could picture me as more
than just a friend, only if...

Water

As the ocean begins to roar under thy moon and thy sands Begin to wash away into thine endless waters.
Let my love for you be taken from your final resting place, forever wandering these endless seas, for I shall never love another maiden again.

To Wear A

To wear a smile,
To hide your pain.
To feel like you always get blamed.
To shed a tear from the inside only, why must I feel so lonely? To
talk to strangers to fill that void, why must I feel so paranoid?
There must be someone who loves me enough to care I've given
up and can't take any more despair.

Emotions

My emotions are all scrambled up inside, I lost a gift I tried to
confide,
Searching the skies and the depths of the sea looking for a gift
that could set me free,
I lost my gift of empathy, oh what could've happened to me?
I can no longer feel what others feel,
I can no longer feel the emotions of thee,
I've lost my gift of sight as well, I can no longer tell such a tale
Your destiny I can't foresee, there's something mystic blinding
me.
Without my gifts of fate, I'm nothing for heaven's sake could I
have lost my gifts because of hate? Or were they merely stolen from
me?
I lost my path and forgot the error of my ways bring back to me
those ancient days,
I call upon the power of empathy and sight bring back to me
what was lost that night,
Bring back to me what is truly mine.

Beauty Within

The beauty within your inner soul is most gratifying and
As my love for you becomes more pure and sustained, I can tell
your love for me slowly fades.

For My Pride

For thou, my pride is greater than my feeling think not that I
don't love you,
Simply because you have not heard from me, but think that I
love you too much, simply because I'm afraid to talk to thee.

A Stranger Past

I take these steps past the path that has been made, thinking of
all the secrets I keep
All of the goodbyes that I back, I am forever broken, take my
busted heart as a Remembrance,
A token
A token of the love we once had and shared but forever gone
now.
Trust you can be glad that we're over, for I am strong now.

Behind These Doors

Behind these doors, death calls to me a whisper so innocent it
sings to me,
Tells me the sins of the fallen, each night holds a new victim and
ends before dawn.

One Day

I came to realize my mind and soul can no longer bare looking down at a world that doesn't have you in it , a lack of words I come to have when you step foot in front of me.
When I watch you lay across those chairs falling asleep my heart stops and somehow starts to accelerate through time.
Waiting for the day when you will be mine.

Reflection

I look at what I thought was my reflection,
But I now know it is not,
He moves the same, sounds the same,
He even looks just like me,
So one can't help but wonder:
Is this a miracle that has been sent to me?
Or a curse reminding me that I could never be free from one,
Who appears to look just like me?
Can I live a life looking like another? Forever being confused as the other?
When can I be free to tell whether this person like me is a blessing or a curse?

Drowning

I drown my sorrows, lock my heart Estranged people we truly are.
My fears of love fill the air, tell me am I supposed to care?
Hate overrules me,
Negativity claims me,
I really don't care if my fear of love shames me for power and fame consumes me.

CHARACTERISTICS

I'm a blunt and honest guy, humble and true, I hope I can prove
I'm this type of a man to you.
I can be persistent and a little annoying at times.
I can be very passionate and very diverse but,
Stating my characteristics won't help us converse so I ask for one
chance,
One date to see if our lives together were meant to be,
Will you do me the honor of going on a date with me?

I Know

I know you notice me as I notice you,
I know you have the same desire as I have for you gaze at me
wanting to say so much but say so little why am I so afraid to talk to
you myself?
Maybe it's the impression you made on me
The emotions we hide but feel for each other will stay hidden
and buried below, underneath the surface.

Boxed In

Boxed in
Locked in
It's hard to breathe
Take this love away from me
I bare the shame of loving another, why must I ponder what life
would be like without my lover?
Why must I wonder such things?
After all, I got my wish that I made upon the stars above I found
my one true love.
But if it's true love, why must I cry Why must I hate myself for
loving you every night?

If I Knew

If I knew then what I know now, I would change nothing , My past made me who I am today and to say I would, I wouldn't have become the man I am today to say I would change it, I wouldn't have grown to be the same.
If I knew then what I know now, I would travel to my past and tell myself I have created a better and brighter future for myself. If I knew then what I know now, I would erase my pain and sorrow from my heart and mind.
If I knew then what I know now...

I Adore

Your eyes sparkle through the night, your skin glows like a fluorescent light, and with your smile, I have come to cherish so... I'm just happy I got to know... Got to know the real you for I adore what you're able to make my heart do.

Lost Love

I'm in love with someone I had but lost , My ego got the best of me, I shouldn't have shoved them off , Right over the cliff my true love fell into another lover's arms, couldn't you imagine such a hell!

I've failed to change for my lover's sake, and it's sad to say how all my motives to try didn't take. I'm in love with someone I had but lost, I tried to move on, and I tried to break free

But

The love I grew for them will forever be everlasting. I'm in love with someone I had but lost.

Pain

I try with all my soul and all my might to mask my pain, With every breath I take, with every move I seem to make I feel like breaking down to cry, for only to then place blame on myself.
My sanity, my strength grows weary
My heart, my mind is torn apart and swept away into   the dust...
With God on my side, I try to fight a good fight But I seem to have lost
when I let you make me feel all this mess.

Promise of Love

I can't promise you the world or
Even the stars above but I promise to love you with the purest of
love.

Suicidal Thoughts

Contemplating thoughts of suicide, this life that I have is not my own, suffocating from the inside. I feel too much and I say too little. Words can't come fast enough to express this mess. I pray to rescue my thoughts from sin. I pray to God to take some of my own pain in. If this is what life truly is, I don't want it. If life after death is truly peaceful, if it brings serenity then I'll love to own it. I was in distress, in pain, and when I'd come to ask for help, no one seemed to care; but people tend to care when they feel like it's something to gain; otherwise they tend to think your pain, your tragedies are sad, pathetic games. But then when I'm gone, what will you all do? Sit here, cry, and claim that you could have been here for my rescue if I had just seemed to tell you, warned you, ha! If you only knew. I pity you even though by the time you read this I'll be gone. It's still you I feel sorry for, for your selfishness caused this one.

Pursuit of Happiness

Life, liberty, and the pursuit of happiness,
Refusing to believe that the bank of happiness is bankrupt:
Demanding the riches of freedom and security of justice that we deserve.
Lord, forgive me for I've been running, running blind, in truth needing freedom to cut me loose.
I've come to break these chains all by myself, won't let all my freedom rot in Hell.
Trying to save enough of my strength to free us. I will not be shackled and locked up against my will. It's ironic that we live in a country that promises freedom for all but none of us are ever really free, are we? A new dawn has set, a new era is upon us.
A time when the government serves only themselves, attacking countries they deem fit. Taking what isn't theirs. For consumption of power, still being labeled generations
Down; we're drowning, can't you see, in a country that claims to be for the land of the free.

Almost a Perfect Dream

I keep dreaming of something I'll never have, the need for True
love is what keeps me awake.
The hunger for a touch is what makes my soul break,
Maybe
I'm dreaming of something I really don't need , Maybe I'm
dreaming of something that'll never be good for me.
Every time I shut my eyes a new character, a new image arrives.
Making me want and feel something that I would've never come
to imagine in this lifetime.

Is It Worth It?

So desperate for affection, you're willing to surround yourself with people that will do nothing more but hold you down and stop you from achieving your goals in life. Is it worth it???

I Was Already Dead

God as my witness, while I sit wrapped up in my towel, crying how everything in my head kept saying overdosing was the easiest

and most painless way to die, and as I cried looking in my bottle, only seeing two pills left,

I wondered if, I were to go to the cabinet and grab something else, would I actually feel myself dying, and no matter what, even an eternity in Hell watching my soul burn from the inside out was

better than living a life I didn't want to live. For a split second without taking anything, I was already dead.

Bipolar Depression

Bipolar depression is a bitch... like Fuck! The only thing I can
think about and feel is how my heart aches from the loss of time
and not having enough accomplished. I can
Tell people my sorrows. I can show others my pain and one
could truly say they understand. I can show you my deepest fears
but you'll think I'm crazy and tell me not to worry, I could
show you the real me and you could find yourself being able to
tell me you love me. Yet I feel so fucking lonely; feeling unlucky and
unblessed to live the life I live; Feeling like I was revived and
saved to watch others live out my heart's desires, feeling like I could
never come to be truly happy... bipolar depression is a bitch.
Wishing there was an on and off switch,
I could come to embrace and see life at its purest, embracing the
beauty within life itself, I could come to embrace the people around
me and the joy they bring to
My heart. Like fuck, I could be as motivated and as ambitious as
my ancestors and I could love as you love me, not worried about
loss of time but stoked to see the future

30

Like fuck... Bipolar depression is a bitch...

A Misguided Thought

Lost all inspiration to write, lost all emotions to feel, more focused on finding a happily ever after. I lost myself going through relationships like a new month catalog of best sellers, never really having to worry how others felt around me, only needing to be concerned with me! Consumed by vanity, I gave my heart to every eligible bachelor that I felt would do justice standing by my side, then healing or holding together a broken heart. So many life
lessons and lost souls passed along this journey of mine that I tend to have left my soul at the starting line and now that I'm near the end there's only one thing I've come to know. My only muse has been my pain, my only inspiration has been my sorrow, and my God-given talent has been nothing more but a simple heartache and failure to hold together any potential relationship. I now know who I am, I now know what I'm meant to be, as everything I've come to know has been nothing less than A Misguided Thought.

Something in My Past

Something in my past
Always keeps me going
To know right from wrong And who to take along.
Something in my past
Keeps me standing strong
From the violence I've seen
To the memories I dream
To the guns that I shoot
To the kids who I root
From my ancestors
To the Queens and Kings who wore crowns.
Something in my past won't let my heart mend Afraid to be
hurt all over again
To share that trust that should grow
How could one ever come to know...?
Something in my past.
To ask the Father; Thou shall you bring someone into my life.
To love, to cherish till death do us part!
Isn't that a start?
Of a new beginning?
To show that you love that man with your whole soul. And not
just half

See it starts out with my past
And now this the beginning
Oh, it's something in my past
That will not let me love this man so unconditionally and I ask:
"Why?"
Something in my past won't let this last
It's easier to run and hide
But now I want to stay and learn To love this man of mine
And sustain till the end of time.
I love you
Maybe, if this is meant to be
We will make it
And if not,
We can learn to be friends.

How I Feel

I've waited forever and a day To say how I feel ,To show you how much my love is real I feel I have loved you a lifetime And it's not enough to satisfy your pride.
We fuss and fight and I wonder: Why do I love you so much? How come I can't let you go?
Well, I am fed up and deserve better and I feel you do too so where do we go from here
You shall go your way and I shall go mine and maybe we can be friends till the end of time but time has come to say goodbye with love from me and love from you
Maybe we can do as mature adults should have done before and just learn to let each other go.
Because sooner Or Later This will soon come to an end!

A Journey

I'm on this journey of solitude, a journey within myself Why am
I so bad? Or am I just so cold-hearted?
Who knows? This journey I'm on is to find myself within my-
self.
Who am I? Strong, Talented, Mindful within means, but who
am I on this journey.
This journey has been a roller coaster... A roller coaster?
You don't understand ,I've loved you ,I've hated you ,I've
despised you , Just to realize you're the one for me. This journey
that I'm on... Has been full of temptation of sex, love, and more!
But through my journey of it all I have passed the test so what is
this quest? My final journey is to respect GOD first. My body,
mind, and soul and make man, Respect ME.
A journey is a lifetime of work whether it's a good woman or a
friend who will listen
A true journey is a never-ending story so to end this journey, I
say this my journey is a long haul and the quest is almost done.

So soon I can say Happy, you're home, and this journey was
worth the wait.

Communication

The thoughts that run through my head are words unexplained trying to catch a voice Sounds, united.
Fighting for someone to understand but wait! Who can have them? No one!
Words scrambled but no sounds of words No one can hear what you don't speak Out of your mouth Communication is the key! We hold words inside Hoping someone understands our silent thoughts But no one does,
Reaching for understanding with words unspoken. Thinking someone can read your mind but they can't! Speak and open your mouth and let sounds roar like thunder.
Communication is the key! Silence is golden, with words unspoken, Thoughts in my head
As I lay in bed wishing my communication had its own form of speech.
Silence, purity, and just knowledge of no sound So, if I speak with my mind, you will understand And if you respond with no words, I will understand Why? Because communication is the key!

He Holds the Future

He is the key to my future
So special and dear
He holds the future which is close and near the love he has shall
never fade
It's unconditional
And never played on a jukebox, on the radio in the shower
On a card table
Just so pure it sees straight through to your soul where it's silver
and gold
Where your mind runs wild
And your heart doesn't grow old.
He can see through me
He knows how I love because
"HE": the creator, King of kings
He holds the key to my heart
My body, my soul, the future
My breath and my awakening every morning is his Thank you,
Lord!
Because only He has the power.
He holds the future in his hands.

Sorry

I'm sorry for the pain I caused
I'm sorry for dropping our conversations without a probable
cause
We've been through so much within this year I'm pretty sure
both our pasts are sure to bring up tears But without a doubt, we
both look toward the future and forget the past I'm so happy 2014
is over at last!
You were my crush, my pride, and joy Happy New Year, love!
Enjoy!

Love

Love is not measured by the physical features a person offers but by the beauty and passion you can see within them when no one else does.

I Dream

I dream of a world full of peace and prosperity I dream of a
world full of enough riches to take care of the homeless and poor
I dream of a world built for you and me
A kingdom just for us
A world this nation has never seen
Let our love flourish and hold together our palace for this dream
is just a dream
Until I find you so we can make it a reality.

Flower Child

From the Heaven to the Earth From the moon and back
I dream of you kissing my neck
My mysterious flower child
So gracious and true
Your eyes see through my soul
My lips yearning to touch yours
But I know what a forbidden sin it is for
A goddess at such rank
But palm to palm
Will rightfully show our affection in this magical place.

Hope

Have you ever had hope?
I did
Hope for riches
Hope for fame
Hope to one day say the same that what I hoped for came true
Do you know hope?
I do.
Hope to know the difference Hope to find myself
But true hope is just having
Faith that it will work out
So I hope that one day I live to see all the things I hoped for.

Sacred Love

My heart and mind belong to thee ,but my soul still screams to
be let free
En-captured in your love, I will not part myself from thee no
matter how much I want to be set free
Because I love thee more than myself
So, my love, you mustn't fear my farewell
For I love you too much to let you go
And I'll stay with you till forever after
Let us die side-by-side near the spot where we met so our love
for each other will remain, and will live after death. Trust me I'm
just as afraid as you to take this leap of faith And the fact that
you have my heart means you're capable of destroying me.

Bleeding Crossroads

A tale of two lovers
A tale of bleeding hearts
They've been through trials, fought through unspeakable hell
It's hard to force true love upon yourself
This book was created for you and me
This book was created to shape our destinies This book is for
those who met at the bleeding crossroads.

Toxic Love

You obviously don't care how I feel or consider the fact that my
love for you is truly pure
And I understand how you may be blinded by the person right
in front of you, but I'm also in your view someone who actually
cares.
Someone who actually wants you for you
Somehow you passed me in your view and chose the other
knowing all they do is hurt you
I guess deep down we like to be toxic.

Supernatural

My vision is going
It's hard to breathe, my future I once saw
I can't foresee, a curse I now have
Makes my power glitch
I wouldn't tell her fortune and that's a sad price I'll now pay I
wish I could go back, rewind to that day
My sight, my vision is what kept me alive all these years but I
know that I'm cursed
My life is starting to give
So as these are my final words
I leave you with this; what's right is right
What's wrong is wrong
But there are exceptions to the supernatural, and that's where I
went wrong.

Not a Love Letter

When the person you love can tell you that you should've
caught that flight back home, that's when you know
the level of love they have for you doesn't compare to the love
you have for them.
He belittles you, makes you feel like you isn't worth nothing,
constantly lies and says he isn't hiding shit but you're not even
allowed to go through his phone.
Got you lying about who you are to him, to his friends and
family, then tells you when you start to complain and express your
emotions that it's all in your head, you're just insecure.
For one, know your worth and no matter how much you love
him, you don't, nor will you or have to ever put up with this bull-
shit. Remember communication is key and
You tried talking to him but he's stubborn and most definitely
set in his own ways. Jae, you don't have to deal with that
If he's not going to work on himself willingly; you need to come
to the realization that you can't force him.
Don't forget this is the same person that told you that his friends
were here before me, fake or not, and I might as well just call myself
replaceable.
Some love, you really let this nigga make you sleep on the couch
because he told you he was sick of sleeping next to you yet after

time you decided to leave him and he begged and pleaded for you to stay, playing off your emotions for him.

Your heart aches from all the fighting, Your emotions matter, You matter.

You're not overweight, yet that's something he says. You shouldn't have to dye down your personality to please him, Know your worth, break free!

I Am Worthy

I asked god to show me if I was worthy
I hoped and prayed that someone heard me
I lost my way, sucked in by temptation
Walking on the edges of a curved path Confused and dazed
Afraid to be hurt and scared of my fate
I asked god to cleanse me
Wash me as if I was a dirty plate
Cleanse the blood off my hands
And give me a new slate
I asked god to hold me
And feed my soul
For my soul feels empty and where my heart is there's a hole
I asked god to forgive me
As I've done so many times before
I apologized for the life he gave me that I've come to mess up
more than once
I asked god to open my eyes
Let me see things for what they really are
Just guide me and help me see
For I'm unaware if I am worthy.

Earth

No matter how much pain Earth comes to bare, she's always full of life.

Lord, Help Me!

Lord, help me. I'm starting to cave in
Heal my mind, body, and soul
Free me from constant sin
I'm struggling right now, only have the energy to let you in
So I bow my head and pray
Help me overcome this pain and cleanse me In the name of the
Father, Son, and Holy Ghost I pray Amen.

Trapped

Trapped and confined by my own mind, constantly wanting to reset time, looking for a way out a way to be free by the gift bestowed in me
Afraid that one day I'll come to fade and be buried by the ravages of time.

Love Has Died

Love has died
And no matter how many times
I've tried, it simply can't be revived
So many lies and single-worded is
Love has died in a relationship between you and I tried but one-
sided compromises
Just weren't right
My pain, my sorrows ignored, my heart on the footsteps of an
open door
Within our home, there was no love
No emotions allowed
To feel was a mistake
To feel would cause me even more pain
To feel would cause an argument and strip my sweet smile and
joy away
Love has died
And no matter how much I pray and hope and try I shouldn't
have to hide my smile, my heart

I shouldn't have to be afraid of what I can and can't say. I
shouldn't have to worry about what I eat now, "Will I gain weight?"
The love I had for you kept me blind
And no matter how much I wanted it not to be true

The love we've had just isn't right
The love we've had has just simply died How come I'm the only
one that tried?
You found every reason to pick a fight
And let's not forget every time I had something to address, it
was always an "I bet" or an "I guess," Like those would suffice?
Fuck! I wanted us and God knows I've tried
You just didn't treat me right
The love we had you killed
And this time I'm man enough not to apologize... Sick of being
criticized
For you, for love, I was blind
But through God I'm constantly reminded of what true love is
like...
No more wasted tears
No more assumptions or being in constant fear I'm free and
finally loved like I shall be
Heard like I shall be, cared for
The love we had has died but through it all
I rediscovered love within God and my own peace of mind.

Best Foot Forward

I'm a poet, that's what I do but not enough words can come to explain how sorry I am that I hurt you, trust is the key to everything and the fact that I kept flaking hasn't at
All contributed to my vision of us wearing those rings. Sometimes I can be a little cheesy.
Hell, I can even stumble over my own two feet but the fact I know you'll come to love me for me will forever keep me trying. I see you as my future and I pray one day you'll come to see me as yours. For what I did yesterday, I'm truly sorry but all will be forgotten by tomorrow as I'll be on one knee by the altar.
I'm constantly running away from all I know, trying to disappear, trying desperately not to be seen yet in the back of my mind I keep asking, "Why isn't anyone stopping me?" Took strangers in just to cast my family out, constantly feeling insecure and overwhelmed by years of pain.
Then I found love, but I'm not really sure I'm just pacing myself, moving in fear.
I'm definitely not the person I used to be.
I have tragically let this illness,
My depression, take hold of me.

Old Me

I pray for guidance, strength, and clarity. Birthday is in 17 days and since the day I've turned 18, I have gone from living a sheltered life to living and learning through real life experiences and as God as
my witness, the knowledge He has bestowed upon me through the few trials that I've been through, I've come to understand and comprehend the true definition of compassion and forgiveness; the difference between listening and comprehending. Most importantly, I've learned that once you come to see life through God's eyes, your entire image, the person you thought you were, the old
you, can totally seem like a distant memory—a fictional character if you will. It is true what they say, you live and learn.

Redemption

Dealing with my troubled mind
I guess this is my punishment for all my crimes, Crimes against
humanity, time and time again racking up and burying myself in
constant sin but I ask you now, God, heal me from within
As you know my heart and I fear condemnation I live with these
thoughts, these memories I know And I understand rightly so
But don't let me be punished in my afterlife too for my heart
still bleeds in this life, wanting and waiting upon it's renew
I repented, I asked you to cleanse my soul
Speaking out loud my tragic sins
Wanting you to erase the filth I took part in
And even though' some aren't even fully my sins the fact I've
come to know what I feel great pain in forgive me, Lord, as I'm
filled with sin
Every thought, every breath that I've taken in make me anew, I
confess all to you
And as I forgive others as you forgave me
Let this be a reminder of how you changed me.

I Am Worthy (Part 2)

The memories I have of us make my heart ache constantly
wanting to press send and see what happens when my message
arrives
But so many what-ifs stop me in my tracks. So much blood still
stained in the carpet is a constant reminder of not to look back.
"It gets better and you'll heal with time!" Things people peri-
odically come to say
But when you once thought this was your forever and this was
the type of love you ever come to know the words "time, healing,
better" seemed to just fade out and disappear within a void.
And no matter how much I try to remind myself I am some-
thing more worthy of what I think I deserve I come to look back at
the memories of my love for you And wonder if my actions
would have been different Would I have been right for you
Or would my heart still remain to be a battleground Constantly
got me questioning if I am worthy When my pain was caused
simply
Because you didn't know how to love me.

Form of Conditions

When did love come in the form of conditions?
When did love become my prison?
Expected to be happy and follow thru
Unjustified reasoning's that make me have to do double takes
when I look at you,
Living as a ghost in my own home, I'd rather come to be alone.
How smug you are thinking I would never leave,
How naive you are thinking your love was enough to keep me.
Rooted on solid ground, is this love?
True love, a love that's worth growing?
From my point of view love doesn't amount to trying but for
your love I have to give up a part of my identity for us to be happy,
but what about my sacrifices? Are they not worthy? Are they not
equal to or more than what I'm asking of you?
When did love come in the form of conditions?

By Grace Through Faith

By grace through faith
Put him behind everything you do
By grace through faith
Honor him and he'll honor you By grace through faith!
God help me patch all my wrongs with all my future rights, God
be my never ending guiding light continue to be my strength , as I
asked for signs and you gave them to me but now I'm confused
on
what to do, what decision shall I choose? What decision aligns
best with you?
But I do know with all these trials and you by my side I'll get
through by grace through faith.

I wanna know

I wanna know what causes a man to lose his soul,
& once lost if my words, if my presence, can restore them.

Beast in Me

Look me in my eyes I'm a beast
When I'm hungry my soul feeds
Fate sealed in stone like Excalibur to be released to cause disaster,
Blooming from the fruits of my tree
An army able to divide the sea
Words conquered and repaired by me
Darkness devoured so light could Rome free what's your answer
when I ask you to join me?

Deprive Them

Deprive them of their basic niceties and their inner core will speak.

Legacy

If I disappeared tomorrow what would be my legacy? Would the world continue to heal without me? Faster or slower? Tell me. Tell me that as people of the human race are we chasing and really trying to achieve the ultimate dream? To give freely, to heal the sick to help those hungry or in need, as an human race are we done taking
resources from a life source that needs replenishing , tell me if I disappeared tomorrow what would the world be?

A Message To You

A collection of thoughts that has plagued my mind,
A world that should believe in healing over-time, let this Mis-
guided Thought be a message to you, words of solace so you know
you're not alone going through the emotional void of pain alone,
let my words of light show you I'll always be here for you.
Here's My Message to you!

What will you decide?

In front of me lye one truth and one lie
In front of me lye the unfulfilled desires of one's life, To achieve
an award like no other! Was the accomplishment ,was your life goal
worth it? you chose to pick a road that was full of lies instead of
basking in your truth. In front of you lye one truth and one lie
on this journey, on this road what will you decide.

Something Real

Don't give another excuse for what I need you to do, I'm so sick,
fed up, tired of you.
Constantly tugging on all my pet peeve's what's wrong with
you?
For all our memories that filled my mind their all outweighed by
your no shows and chronic lies, a fool I am for sticking by your side.
I shouldn't want or crave another but it's you, your behavior!
Something about you gets me in an endless loop to be hurt, cry,
and constantly mope over you, this isn't love it's toxic and I've had
enough.
Let another love me for more than what I have to show, let
another love me for something I didn't come to know or under-
stand myself, let another love me! Better yet let them understand
me , as I crave to be understood, crave to be held, I crave for
some-
thing more than the prison we built for ourselves behind these
four walls, I pray for something real , I pray for true love.

Unanswered call

An unanswered call that weakens me in the knees, an unanswered prayer that got me questioning if you can hear me, moving by faith within I'll find my strength!
For I'm hoping you can hear me.

I am who I am

I am who I am,
No matter the flaw,
I am who I am,
Warts and all behind my face is true beauty,
Behind these scars you'll come to see fully,
See me for who I am,
See me for my worth,
See me for my heart, I am who I am, No matter the scars,
Behind my face is true beauty.

Death seeks a Bride

If you read my work you would know that death loves to call to
me
A whisper in the dark that longs for me
Within my mind I ask for help
But out loud around my peers I'm constantly giving more of me
If you read my work you would know death calls to me, to just
wake up comes to drain me
A passion and possession of love is what I hope to gain but to
just get there the loops I got to jump through is just insane
Like fog in the night, I'm blind to what I can't see, hoping and
praying god comes rescue me.
A link I share with the dead, the pain I hold deep inside, and
death calls to me for death seeks a bride.

Looking Glass

Through the looking glass you see a man
Able to hold and take care of his own
But within his mind he suffers alone
Told to keep working and pray the pain away
But the thing he come to know is pain and the more he pray the
more his faith fades,
Scared and lost he took his own life
Because his parents just kept giving him tools instead of check-
ing on his mind.
Inspired and wrote for a lost pastor's son.

Stolen in Time

Give me back what is mine
Give me back what was stolen in time As I fight to protect my
mind!

H.A.T.E

Hate an easy thing to do
Hate a word when mad becomes you
Hate a feeling that consumes your soul Hate a word you have to
let go!

Definition of Love

What's your definition of love?
To love me at my finest hour
To love me for all the joyful things I didn't sour What's your
definition of love?
To love me when I'm only right,
To love me when you're in my arms at night.
What's your definition of love?
To see me when someone else sees me
To love me when someone else wants me Tell me what's your
definition of love?
For all the things I do right I have done just the same number of
things wrong.
Tell me what's your definition of love?

No Escape

Either way I'm drowning,
I have no escape,
Constantly trying to be positive and remember to pray, but with
no physical support I've been falling short on my praying days.
Overwhelmed at its core, tired and drained but because I'm 24 I
must not know what being buried under the shackles of time, stuck
and confined with a generational curse that only your trying to
break . I need a break, a break to heal, time to rest and wake up
with
fresh eyes as I dream of creating a world anew. I need my faith
refilled and my mind at ease. I need family support to help me
breathe.
I know with god my pain should seem more at ease but truth-
fully I'm unaware if god is hearing me.
Either way I'm drowning trying to survive with my faith in god I
hope I make it because I can no longer take it!

Do you?

Do you still want me as I want you?
Do you crave my kisses as I crave you?!
This is what love , do! Turns a person like me into a sucker for
you, day or night- I'll stay by your side.

Jaelyn D. Jordan likes to think of Himself as a creative, charismatic individual who finds solace in his own writing and hopes that others will as well, as he expresses love, lust, and loss through his work. He Restarted writing poetry at the age of sixteen and could have never guessed then that this was something she wanted to do career-wise. After two failed attempts trying to self-publish with two individual companies, Mr.Jordan has
successfully founded his own Publication House, Record Label & Fashion line all to inspire and bring light to Mental Health Awareness as he personally suffers from Manic Depression.

" A Misguided Thought " was crafted so none us ever has to feel alone, trapped, or lost in our Thoughts.

www.Amisguidedt
hought.com